Global Issues

DRUGS

Jonathan Rees

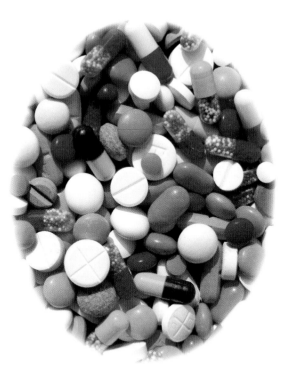

WALRUS

B O O K S

GLOBAL ISSUES

DRUGS   **EQUAL OPPORTUNITIES**   **RACISM**   **TERRORISM**

Visit our website at www.whitecap.ca.

Library and Archives Canada Cataloguing in Publication

Rees, Jonathan, 1967-
        Drugs / Jonathan Rees.
(Global Issues)

ISBN 1-55285-743-3

        1. Drugs--Juvenile literature.   2. Drug abuse--Juvenile literature.

I. Title. II. Series: Global issues (North Vancouver, B.C.)

HV5809.5.R43 2006   j362.29   C2005-905630-4

Commissioning Editor: Jason Hook
Designer: Jane Hawkins
Consultant: Jim Mulligan and Peter Hayes, CSV
Picture Researcher: Lynda Lines
Produced by Roger Coote Publishing, Gissing's Farm, Fressingfield, Suffolk IP21 5SH, U.K.

The Publisher acknowledges the financial support of the Government of Canada through the Book Publishing Industry Development Program for our publishing activities.

Printed and bound in China
10 9 8 7 6 5 4 3 2 1

Picture Acknowledgements
We wish to thank the following individuals and organizations for their help and assistance, and for supplying material in their collections: Associated Press 17 (Gael Cornier), 21 (Apichart Weerawong), 27 (Elaine Thompson), 28 (René Macura), 33 (James A Finley), 37 (Kevin Frayer), 41 (Peter Dejong), 44 (Mary Ann Chastain); Corbis 12 (Sean Sexton Collection), 13 (Bettmann); Health Promotion England 29; Hutchison Library 39 (Susan Dent); John Birdsall Photography 35, 43; MPM Images 1, 4 (Corel), 34; Panos 5 bottom (Dermot Tatlow), 8 (Neil Cooper), 10 (Gareth Wyn Jones), 19 (Morris Carpenter), 23 (Martin Lueders), 36 (Gisele Wulfsohn); Popperfoto front cover (Reuters), 3 (Reuters), 5 middle, 11 (Andy Solomon/Reuters), 14 (Reuters), 15 (Reuters), 18 (Reuters), 20 (Reuters), 24 (Reuters), 25 (Reuters), 26 (Reuters), 31 (Reuters), 38 (Reuters), 40 (Reuters), 42 (Reuters), 45; Rex Features 5 top (Sipa), 6 (David White), 9 (Neil Stevenson), 16, 22 (Mansell/ Timepix), 30, 46 (Sipa); Science Photo Library 7, 47 (Hank Morgan); Topham Picturepoint 32. Artwork by Michael Posen. The pictures used in this book do not show the actual people named in the case studies in the text.

CONTENTS

Suzie's Story

Eighteen-year-old Suzie leads a life like that of many other teenagers in Britain. She is studying for tests later in the year and hopes to go to college if she gets the right grades. She has many friends and a loving family, and plays soccer for her school team. Until recently, however, Suzie was also one of the estimated 500, 000 people in Britain who regularly take the drug ecstasy.

"THE FIRST DRUG I tried was cannabis, when I was fifteen. A friend let me smoke a joint, but I didn't really like it very much. I kept smoking cannabis for a few months because a couple of my friends were really into it, and I just sort of went along with what they were doing. But I found that I was losing interest in things I enjoyed, such as sports, and sometimes I just couldn't be bothered to do my homework. I realized I had to stop taking the drug as I had tests coming up. I'm really glad I did, as my two friends eventually dropped out of school completely.

Last year, though, I started going clubbing. To begin with, I never went anywhere near drugs, though there were loads of them around and people kept offering them to me. I just didn't want to go down that road again. On my last birthday, though, I got quite drunk and decided to take an ecstasy pill, as it was a special occasion. After that I took ecstasy most times I went to a club.

It seemed great fun for a time, and I felt part of the 'in' crowd. But after a while I thought that I couldn't have fun unless I was taking drugs. I changed my mind after a couple of months. Ben, one of my new friends, suddenly stopped going clubbing. When I asked him why, he said he just couldn't handle it any more. He'd been taking ecstasy for the past three years, and he was sure it was making him depressed. He said that each week, a couple of days after taking a pill he felt so down he couldn't get out of bed. He'd been to see his doctor and they both agreed that he had to stop taking drugs and move on with his life.

Although I never had any bad experiences like Ben's I decided it was time for me to stop taking drugs. I still go to clubs, and I enjoy it just as much as I ever did. You don't need to get 'high' on drugs to have an amazing time. And I'm working really hard for my tests. I know that my future doesn't have to have anything to do with drugs, and I'm just grateful I never got into any real trouble when I used them."

Drugs in three countries

Suzie is just one of millions of people around the world whose lives are involved with and affected by drugs in some way.

PAKISTAN
Nazir is addicted to opium. Five years ago, after his son was killed in a robbery, he turned to the drug in an attempt to overcome his grief. It did not work, and now he struggles to hold down a job and is desperate to kick his habit.

United States
Jenny takes the anti-depressant drug Prozac. "Sometimes I can't cope with the kids and my job," she says. "When things get tough, the doctor makes sure I get enough pills to help me for a few months. I'm not addicted, though. I can stop and start them when I like."

CHINA
Jiang owns a market stall in Beijing, selling herbs and other plants for medicine. Many people in the city buy these ingredients from Jiang, then use them to prepare their own herbal remedies.

What Are Drugs?

A drug is something that changes the way your body works. There are thousands of different kinds of drug. Many are made from plants or from substances found in plants. Others are made synthetically, using chemicals in a laboratory.

People take drugs of abuse in a wide variety of situations such as this "rave." Dance music is closely associated with the taking of the drug ecstasy.

SOME DRUGS ARE used by people to change their mood and the way they feel about things. Some, such as alcohol, are legal in most countries. Others, such as ecstasy, are illegal. They are known as drugs of abuse, or recreational drugs.

Other drugs are medicinal. They can change the way you feel pain or help your body to fight illness. Some medicinal drugs, such as painkillers, can be bought from a drugstore. Others, such as antibiotics used to fight infections, are mainly available after seeing a doctor.

Each year, new drugs are discovered or invented. Sometimes these are drugs of abuse, but most often they are medicinal drugs produced by pharmaceutical companies to improve healthcare.

What drugs of abuse are there?

There are many different kinds of drugs of abuse. Worldwide, the most commonly used are amphetamines, cannabis, cocaine, ecstasy, heroin, and opiates. Some of these drugs, such as amphetamines and heroin, can also be used as medicines.

Drugs of abuse are sometimes described as "hard" or "soft." Hard drugs, such as heroin and cocaine, are considered to be more dangerous and addictive. Cannabis

Drugs of abuse come in many forms, including pills, powders, liquids, and plant extracts. This drugs haul includes cannabis seeds and resin, magic mushrooms, cocaine, amphetamines, and ecstasy.

(also called pot, marijuana, and hash) is described as a soft drug, because it is less addictive. But the terms "hard" and "soft" are not accurate scientific descriptions, and the long-term dangers of a drug such as cannabis are difficult to measure.

What medicinal drugs are there?

The term medicinal drugs covers a huge range of products. Worldwide, the most widely used are painkillers and antibiotics, which sell in their hundreds of millions each year. In the 1990s, three specific drugs — the anti-depressant Prozac, a drug called Zantac used for treating stomach ulcers, and the anti-impotence drug Viagra — were the best-selling brand-name drugs. Millions of dollars are spent each year on developing new drugs and testing them so that they can be used safely. Even so, there are still concerns about how safe or addictive certain medicinal drugs really are.

How are drugs taken?

Drugs of abuse come in a range of forms. Cannabis is usually smoked with tobacco in a cigarette. Heroin can be smoked, inhaled, or injected into the bloodstream using a syringe. Cocaine comes as a powder, which is inhaled through the nose. Other drugs of abuse, such as ecstasy, are taken as pills.

Many medicinal drugs come in the form of pills or liquid medicines, which are swallowed. Some, such as the insulin needed by diabetics, are injected.

Cannabis sativa *is a plant grown all around the world and put to many uses, including the production of drugs. The plant thrives in many different climates.*

What are the effects of drugs of abuse?

Different drugs of abuse have very different effects, and the effects can vary from person to person. Drugs known as stimulants speed up how the mind and body work, while drugs called sedatives slow things down. Drugs called hallucinogens alter how a user senses things, and trigger hallucinations — seeing, hearing, or feeling things that are not really there.

Cannabis is the most commonly used drug in Australia, Western Europe and the U.S.. It comes from the plant *Cannabis sativa*. Cannabis can take the form of a dried leaf ("grass") or a solid resin ("hash"). It is a mild sedative, and after smoking it people commonly feel relaxed and happy. But users can also feel panicky or paranoid.

Cocaine, a white powder that acts as a strong stimulant, comes from the coca plant. Users feel exhilarated and have a sense of fearlessness. Other less pleasant effects can include a racing heart and insomnia. Heating cocaine with baking soda and water forms a drug called crack. This comes in small, rock-like pieces, which are usually smoked. The effects are similar to cocaine but tend to be more intense and short-term. Cocaine can also be used in medicine as an anesthetic.

Amphetamines, also known as speed, are stimulants. The effects are similar to cocaine, but tend to be less intense and to last longer. Amphetamines are a synthetic drug, produced from chemicals in a laboratory.

Ecstasy is a synthetic stimulant and mild hallucinogen. It can make users feel energetic and very friendly. They may also experience a dangerous increase in body temperature.

Heroin is a powerful sedative. Users feel an intense euphoria and sense of well-being, but first-time users are often violently sick. Heroin, opium, and morphine are all made from opium poppies and are known as opiates.

LSD (Lysergic acid diethylamide) is a hallucinogen. It produces hallucinations which can vary from fascinating visions and insights to terrible nightmares.

There are numerous other drugs of abuse, and also substances that are used as drugs. Fumes from solvents such as glue, and chemicals such as gasoline, are sometimes inhaled to make the user hallucinate or have a brief "high."

What are the immediate after-effects?

With most of the drugs listed above, the effects wear off after a few hours. With cannabis, there are no significant immediate after-effects besides an increased appetite. After taking cocaine or ecstasy, though, the user is likely to feel tired and depressed. This can sometimes last for a few days. The long-term effects of drugs are dealt with in the following chapters.

Many club-goers regularly take stimulant drugs such as ecstasy and amphetamines.

Why do people use drugs of abuse?

Nearly all teenagers have heard of drugs of abuse and their effects and know that many people around the world use them. It is hardly surprising, then, that they become interested in drugs and curious to find out how drugs make you feel.

Some people imagine that taking drugs might be an enjoyable experience and a fun thing to do. Others are drawn to drugs because they are illegal and they feel that taking them is rebellious. They might also like the idea of doing something that is thought of as being dangerous. People also start taking drugs because of peer pressure. If their friends or family members are taking drugs, they feel they should follow the crowd and experiment themselves.

Some of the highest rates of drug abuse in the developed world occur in inner city areas where there is high unemployment and poor housing. People start using drugs because they are leading difficult lives and they feel it is a way to escape their everyday problems. However, drug abuse is not restricted to only certain areas.

Drug users gather at a disused railroad station in Switzerland. Drug abuse is not a problem which is confined to poor countries or regions.

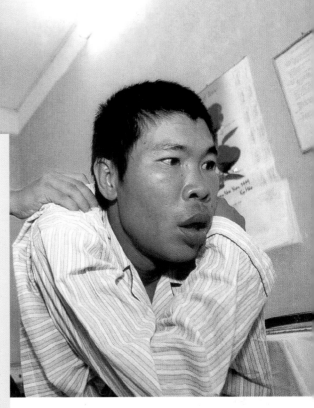

A heroin addict in Vietnam suffers the horrifying withdrawal symptoms which result from trying to quit this highly-addictive drug.

In Britain, a 1999 Home Office survey found that the rural counties of Devon and Cornwall were among those with above average drug use. Young people who lived in these rural areas commonly complained that there was nothing to do and that they turned to drugs because they were bored.

Drug use tends to increase where there are particular problems, such as war or poor living conditions. In Iran, for example, it is estimated that 10 percent of the population regularly takes drugs. This is blamed on poverty, the low cost of drugs in the region and a ban on the consumption of alcohol in the country.

Are drugs addictive?

Some drugs, including cocaine and heroin, are highly addictive. This means that after a certain amount of use your body or brain starts to need the drug to function normally, and you start to crave the drug when you stop using it. With some drugs, such as crack cocaine, it is possible to become addicted after trying the drug just a few times.

Alcohol and tobacco may be legal in many countries, but it should not be forgotten that they too are addictive drugs. This is why many people who smoke or drink regularly experience great difficulty when they try to give up the habit.

Who Takes Drugs Of Abuse?

People have been using recreational drugs for thousands of years. In 8000 B.C., people in Central America were using beans from the mescal plant as a stimulant. A form of this drug, mescalin, is still used by people today. There is also evidence from 5,000 years ago of cannabis use in central Asia and China.

Opium smokers in China in the nineteenth century. Smoking opium was a popular activity in the country for many years.

DEBATE - Does history show that taking recreational drugs is normal?

- Yes. If people were taking recreational drugs thousands of years ago, surely it is just a normal activity like eating and drinking. Why shouldn't we do it today?

- No. Drugs were used in the past because of ignorance. Today, we are better educated about the damage drugs do to our minds and bodies.

STONE TABLETS FROM the ancient Sumerian civilization (in modern-day Iraq) indicate that opium was used for pain relief and as a relaxant around 4000 B.C. The use of opium spread around the world. In modern times, smoking opium became a popular recreation in Europe in the seventeenth century. European traders introduced the habit to China, where addiction became so widespread that opium was banned by the government.

A portrait of Samuel Taylor Coleridge. Like some modern musicians and writers, parts of his work may have been written under the influence of recreational drugs.

Samuel Taylor Coleridge

Many modern-day artists have admitted to taking drugs, but they are not doing anything new. The poet Samuel Taylor Coleridge (1772–1834) was one of many historic figures known to have smoked opium. It is said that he wrote one of his most famous poems, *Kubla Khan*, after having taken the drug.

Britain fought two wars with China over control of the lucrative opium market, from 1839–42 and 1856–60. This resulted in defeat for the Chinese, Britain taking control of Hong Kong, and the opium trade continuing to flourish. By 1900, when opium was still legal in the U.S. and Europe, there were at least 200,000 Americans addicted to drugs which contained opium.

How did modern drug use develop?

The leaves of the coca shrub have been used as a stimulant in some places in the world for over 4,000 years, and in 1865 cocaine was first extracted from them. By the 1970s, cocaine had become popular with regular drug-takers.

Heroin was also developed in the nineteenth century, originally to help people addicted to a drug called morphine. Doctors soon realized that the new drug was even more of a problem than the one it had replaced, and heroin addiction has today become a major problem.

In the 1960s, with the growing importance of youth culture, the use of cannabis and LSD increased. Then the explosion of dance music in the late 1980s led to a new craze with "dance drugs" such as ecstasy. The nature of taking drugs has changed continually over the centuries. It may well change even more in the future.

Who uses what in the Americas?

In the U.S. in the late 1970s, 14 percent of the population took drugs of abuse. By 1999, this figure had fallen to 6 percent, but the U.S. was home to some 810,000 heroin users.

South America, where most of the world's cocaine is produced, has the largest problem with the drug after the U.S. In Argentina, for example, 2.3 percent of adults are regular users of cocaine.

The United Nations Drug Control Program (UNDCP) has noted an increase in the use of cocaine in Central America. It blames this increase on the continuing trafficking of drugs through this area. But overall drug use is relatively low compared to North and South America. In Mexico, for example, only 0.5 percent of the population regularly uses drugs.

(Sources: Barry McCaffrey, Chief U.S. Drugs Advisor; UNDCP; U.S. State Department)

Who uses what in Africa?

Recreational drug use in South Africa is steadily increasing, with a sedative called methaqualone being the most widely used. Across the rest of Africa, however, drug use is below average compared to the rest of the world. Only 0.3 percent of adults have used cocaine, and 0.02 percent have taken ecstasy. Only cannabis is regularly used across the continent, with 5.8 percent of adults using it.

(Source: UNDCP)

Who uses what in Asia?

By the late 1990s, officials in China estimated that there were at least 500,000 heroin addicts in the country. In Pakistan, there are nearly four million people addicted to heroin and opium. This figure is said to be increasing by 100,000 per year. Pakistan produces very little opium but is flooded with the drug from neighboring Afghanistan, the world's largest producer.

(Source: BBC Online)

The Colombian authorities arrest one of the many traders suspected of trafficking drugs through South America.

Afghan farmers extracting opium from poppies. Opium production is one of the most profitable occupations in Afghanistan.

Who uses what in Australia?

According to a 1998 survey, nearly 40 percent of Australians over the age of 14 have used cannabis at least once. Heroin use is on the rise in Australia, with 2.2 percent of all Australians reported to have experimented with heroin at least once.

(Source: Australian Institute of Health and Welfare (AIHW))

Who uses what in Europe?

A recent European Union Drugs Agency survey found that throughout Europe, use of almost all drugs, except ecstasy, is on the increase. Forty percent of 16-year-olds in Britain have tried cannabis in the last year, compared with just 5 percent in Portugal and Finland. There are over a million regular cannabis users in Britain, with only Denmark having a higher rate of use.

(Source: European Monitoring Center for Drugs and Drug Addiction (EMCDDA))

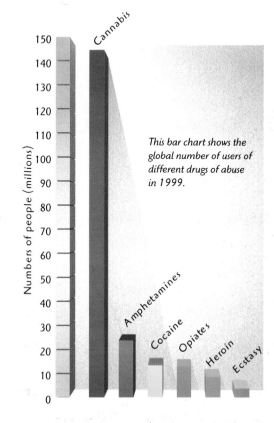

This bar chart shows the global number of users of different drugs of abuse in 1999.

Are Drugs Of Abuse Harmful?

Worldwide, at least 50,000 people die each year as a result of taking drugs. Most of these deaths are a result of heroin and opium use. But the risks involved in taking drugs are not just about whether they kill you or harm your body. Drug abuse can also affect how your mind works, and the effects can be permanent.

Sorted.

Just one Ecstasy tablet took Leah Betts.

MAIDEN

The death of Leah Betts in 1995, from taking ecstasy, led to a high-profile campaign in Britain warning of the dangers of this particular drug.

WHEN SOMEONE TAKES a drug, the immediate side-effects can be very serious. In the case of ecstasy, the drug interferes with the body's ability to regulate temperature. If a user does not drink enough fluids, this can result in overheating and sometimes death. Cannabis is known as a mild drug, but it too can be dangerous.

When someone smokes it, the drug lowers their blood pressure. In some people this can lead to a stroke (bleeding in the brain) or heart failure.

With some drugs, overdose is the main risk. This is certainly the case with heroin. Sometimes the effects cause the user to forget how much they have taken.

Drug users exchange syringes in Lisbon, Portugal, June 2000, at a mobile centre set up to reduce the dangers of infection caused by dirty needles. The government regards drug users as victims who require daily help, not punishment (see panel on page 23).

In other cases, a drug is not pure as dealers mix in other substances, so that they can make more money from selling the same amount of the drug. If these substances are poisonous, the results can be fatal.

Glue-sniffing

Solvent abuse or "glue-sniffing" is a worldwide problem. Since 1971, in Britain alone, it has caused more than 1,500 deaths. Even now, solvent abuse accounts for about 1 percent of all deaths of 10–14 year olds. In Britain, children under 16 cannot buy products that could be used for sniffing, but most homes have cupboards full of dangerous chemicals.

If someone injects drugs there is also the risk of contracting diseases such as HIV (Human Immunodeficiency Virus) and hepatitis. Portugal has the highest HIV infection rate in Europe, with intravenous drug use accounting for 55 percent of all cases.

What are the psychological risks?

According to the *British Journal of Psychiatry*, there is evidence that using cannabis can have a serious effect on mental health. For some people, taking the drug can lead to psychosis (confusion and an inability to understand what is happening) and even to the serious mental disorder called schizophrenia.

Other drugs can also cause mental problems. Some LSD users report flashbacks to "trips" (the feelings you get when using the drug), sometimes many years after taking the drug. And many users of ecstasy report the "midweek blues," feelings of depression which may last for a few days after taking the drug. There are also reports that ecstasy can cause long-term or permanent depression and memory loss.

How do drugs affect society?

People who take drugs are not the only victims of drug abuse. Heroin and cocaine addicts can need from U.S.$14 000 to $56 000 each year to feed their habits. Most addicts cannot afford this, so they raise the money through crime. In Britain, the National Association for the Care and Resettlement of Offenders (NACRO) said that, people trying to get money for drugs committed one-third of all burglaries, street robberies, and thefts in 1999. The problem is a worldwide one. In Russia, the Public Health Ministry estimated that there were two million

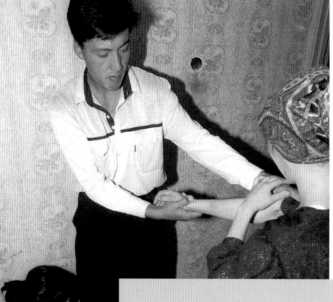

An anti-drugs officer in Kyrgyzstan checks the arm of a drug addict to see whether she has been injecting herself with heroin.

Drugs and pregnancy

Sally lives in Boston, Mass. She became addicted to crack when she was 17 and also began taking heroin. When she became pregnant at 21, she knew that she should stop taking drugs. But she found giving up crack too difficult and carried on taking it until her baby was born. Her son Sean is now three. He is lucky that he seems to have no permanent health problems. Many babies born to addict mothers have heart and lung defects. They are also likely to be addicted to the drugs their mother took when pregnant and to suffer withdrawal symptoms after they are born.

Source: USA Today

South African police arrest a crime suspect. Nearly half of all those arrested in the country test positive for drugs.

addicts in 2000, and that there were over 200,000 drug-related crimes in that same year. In South Africa in 2001, a study showed that more than 45 percent of crime suspects tested positive for at least one drug of abuse shortly after they were arrested.

Drug abuse puts extra strain on health services and costs countries millions of dollars in education and policing. The United Nations Office for Drug Control and Crime Prevention (UNODCCP) estimated the cost of drug abuse to Australia in 1992 at nearly U.S.$1 billion and to the U.S. economy in the same year at a staggering U.S.$98 billion.

Do drugs affect driving?

Over the past few years, people have grown more aware of the dangers of drinking and driving. However, the use of drugs while driving has increased. In 1994, a U.S. study of dangerous drivers found that over half of those who were not intoxicated with alcohol were under the influence of cocaine or cannabis.

A 1999 British report by the Automobile Association and the Association of Chief Police Officers found that in the previous 15 years, the number of people who had died in road accidents as a result of taking drugs had risen from 3 percent to 18 percent of total road deaths. Police forces around the world are so worried about the problem that they are introducing detection kits to test whether drivers have been taking drugs.

What is the world trade in illegal drugs?

In 2000, a United Nations (UN) study found that the value of the trade in illegal drugs around the world could be as high as U.S.$400 billion. This is an astonishing 8 percent of total world trade. It means the drugs trade is larger than the steel or motor trade, and about equal to the oil or tourism trades.

How does the drug trade affect countries?

Morocco, in North Africa, is one of the largest cannabis producers in the world. It is said to earn U.S.$2 billion annually from producing the drug. In 1999, Colombia, in South America, actually decided to include the income from drugs of abuse in its official trade figures. It estimated that the value of this trade was about U.S.$448 million. This boosted Colombia's annual trade figures by about 1 percent.

Growing demand for heroin

Most of the heroin that is sold in Britain and the U.S. comes from poppies grown in Afghanistan. Since the terrorist attacks on New York on September 11, 2001, and the ensuing war in Afghanistan, the price of heroin in the country has halved from U.S.$400 to $200 per kilogram. This drop in price is likely to lead to lower worldwide prices and a greater popular demand for the drug.

In 1998, Colombian police seize 17 tonnes of cannabis bound for Italy, just a small percentage of the total smuggled around the world.

According to a report in Britain's *Observer* newspaper in 1999, cannabis is the biggest farm crop, by value, in the American states of Alaska, Kentucky, Virginia, and California. In Britain, government figures show that the illegal drug industry is worth up to U.S.$11.9 billion every year. This figure includes the money involved in buying, selling, and manufacturing drugs—and is equivalent to about 1 percent of the country's total trade.

How can countries change?

Some countries choose to move their economies away from reliance on the drugs trade. In 2000, the government of Myanmar (Burma) announced plans to depopulate one of the world's biggest opium-growing areas in an attempt to halt heroin production. This would mean relocating 50,000 villagers in the remote Shan State, where little but opium poppies could be grown, to new agricultural areas near Thailand. In Pakistan, official figures show that in response to government efforts, opium production dropped from 700 tons in 1979 to around 10 tons in 1999.

Attempts to stop drug production are not always so successful. To help stop cheap cocaine coming into the country, the U.S. has been supporting anti-drugs operations in Colombia. As a result, production of cocaine is starting to decrease there. In neighboring Peru, however, there are signs that cocaine production is beginning to rise again.

Soldiers and villagers use sticks to chop down opium poppies in Shan State, Myanmar in January 2000. The government of Myanmar stated that more than 1,000 acres of opium fields were destroyed that year.

Should Drugs Be Legalized?

Until the late nineteenth century, there were no illegal drugs. Opium was widely available in the U.S. and Britain and was an ingredient in "soothing" children's medicines. Cocaine may have been one of the original ingredients used in Coca-Cola.

IN 1878, HOWEVER, Britain passed the first Opium Act, in an attempt to limit access to the drug and reduce the number of people taking it. Over the following years, more and more laws were passed. Eventually, most drugs that are now considered drugs of abuse were outlawed.

How are drugs classified?

Many countries, including the U.S., Britain, France, and the Netherlands, classify drugs according to how dangerous they are. Punishments for selling or using the more dangerous drugs are automatically more severe. Other countries, such as Sweden and

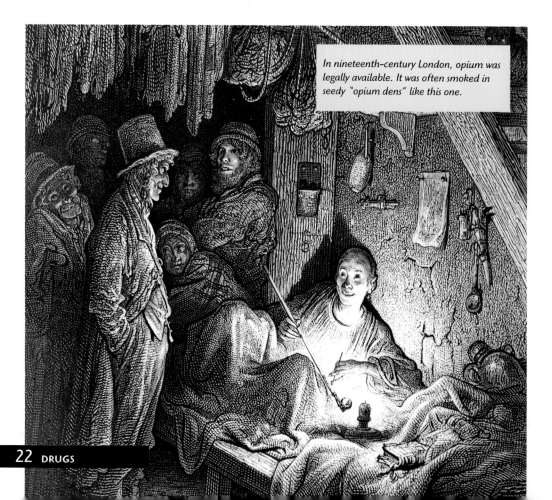

In nineteenth-century London, opium was legally available. It was often smoked in seedy "opium dens" like this one.

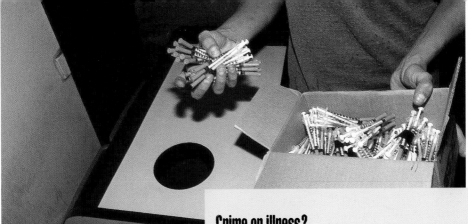

A needle bank in Chicago, 1997. In many cities around the world, drug addicts can now swap used syringes for new ones, which greatly reduces the danger of infection.

Crime or illness?

In Portugal, drug addiction is treated as an illness rather than a crime, and in July 2001 the Portuguese government decriminalized all personal drug use. Another indication of this growing trend was the opening of Australia's first legal heroin–injecting room, in May 2001. Addicts can go there to take their drugs, safe from the dangers of infected needles.

Germany, do not automatically distinguish between different drugs, but leave it for courts to decide how serious they consider a particular offence.

In Britain, drugs such as heroin, cocaine, LSD, and ecstasy are known as Class A drugs. Conviction for possession can lead to a maximum seven-year prison sentence and a fine. Class B drugs include amphetamines (speed) and Class C drugs include tranquillizers and cannabis. With Class C drugs, the maximum sentence for possession is two years. Sentences for dealing drugs are always much more severe.

In the U.S., all drugs, including medicinal drugs, are given one of five categories. Category One represents the most dangerous drugs, while Category Five includes over-the-counter medicines. In almost every state,

a criminal conviction for a drugs offense also brings with it the loss of the offender's voting rights.

Why are some drugs illegal?

Should taking drugs be a matter of personal choice? Or do governments have a duty to use laws to stop people taking drugs? Some people argue that if drugs were legal, then more people would become users. They say this is reason enough for them to remain illegal. After all, it is a fact that drugs do kill and harm some users.

Others argue that some users take drugs because they like to break the law, and making drugs legal would make them less attractive. Some argue that taking drugs is just entertainment and, as it is statistically safer than pursuits such as driving and smoking, there is no reason for it to be illegal.

U.S. customs officers guard a ship seized in 1995 carrying 12 tons of cocaine.

Would legalizing drugs reduce crime?

About U.S.$20 billion is spent each year on enforcing drugs laws in the U.S., and one million arrests are made on drugs charges. In the U.K., two-thirds of the money that the government gives to tackling drugs issues is spent on law enforcement, leaving only a small proportion for drugs education and rehabilitation programs.

Because drugs are illegal, every time someone takes them they are effectively a criminal. Should drugs be legalized, or at least decriminalized, so that drug users are no longer seen as criminals? This would at least save the money that is spent on policing.

Beach seizure

The seizure of cocaine worth U.S.$127.5 million on a remote Australian beach in 2001 highlighted the massive scale of drug smuggling around the world. In 1999, there were an estimated 23 billion drug doses (one dose meaning how much a drug user takes each time) seized worldwide. But although police and customs officials find large amounts of illegal drugs every year, it has been estimated that over 90 percent of shipments slip through the net and make it through onto the open market.

Source: CNN and UNDCP

How could decriminalizing drugs help?

It has long been argued that crimes such as theft are such big problems in today's world because drugs are illegal. Francis Wilkinson, a former senior police officer in Wales, said in 2001 that heroin should be legalized in a bid to reduce street crime. He noted that because the drug is against the law, users have to find huge amounts of money to buy their drugs. Theft is usually the only way to do this.

Edward Ellison, the former head of the Anti-Drugs Squad in London, agreed. He said that he wanted to see all drugs legalized. This would remove the profit from organized criminals, who make so much money out of dealing in drugs. He also suggested that drugs should be manufactured by reputable companies. The companies could produce good-quality drugs, which could then be sold to users at reasonable prices.

DEBATE - Does banning drugs work?

In the 1920s, the production and consumption of alcohol was banned in the U.S.. This was known as Prohibition. During Prohibition, crime rates soared, but fell when the ban was lifted and alcohol became legal again. Would crime rates fall in the same way if drugs were legalized today?

- Yes. Prohibition clearly shows that legalizing drugs would lead to a fall in crime rates.
- No. Criminals will use any excuse to make money. If drugs were legalized, they would simply turn to different forms of crime.

Protesters in favour of legalizing cannabis block the streets of Sydney, Australia, in 1999.

Attitudes to cannabis vary between countries. At this cannabis café in Amsterdam, Holland, cannabis growers enter their plants into a competition without fear of breaking the law.

Is cannabis a special case?

One drug in particular is discussed when people talk about making drugs of abuse legal. Cannabis is used by millions of people around the world, and some countries have started to relax their laws in response to this.

Since the 1970s, people have been able to buy cannabis from coffee shops in Holland. The drug is still illegal, but the authorities do not prosecute anyone who has only a small amount of it. In Switzerland, cannabis weed can be sold in shops, but only if it is sold as products such as "tea" and "scent sachets"—but not as a drug. And in 2001, the Belgian government announced that it would move toward the decriminalizing of cannabis.

In 2000, a Police Foundation report in the UK suggested that cannabis should be downgraded from a Class B to a Class C drug, making arrest or imprisonment for using the drug very unlikely. It said that the harsh penalties for possessing and taking the drug were more harmful than the drug itself.

The government initially rejected the proposal. But in 2001, the Home Secretary went ahead and downgraded cannabis to a Class C drug. He said that the aim of the policy was to free the police to concentrate their time on dealing with harder drugs, such as heroin and cocaine. But he added that he had no intention of decriminalizing cannabis.

The debate continues. Some think that governments which are lenient on soft drugs are encouraging drug use, and that this will inevitably lead to more users. Others say that the law against cannabis should be completely scrapped and that the drug should be as legal as tobacco and alcohol.

Is cannabis a medicinal drug?

At the same time as announcing the reclassification of cannabis, the British Home Secretary stated that if clinical trials were successful, the law would allow the use of cannabis-based medicinal drugs. Sufferers of conditions such as multiple sclerosis and arthritis have said for years that cannabis is an effective treatment for the pain they endure. They have argued that they should be able to obtain the drug legally. In July 2001, Canada became the first country to legalize medicinal cannabis.

DEBATE – Should cannabis be legal?

- No. Cannabis is a "gateway drug," with users more likely to move on to more dangerous drugs. Sweden, which has strict laws against all drugs (including cannabis) has one of the lowest rates of hard-drug use in Europe.

- Yes. According to the European Monitoring Center for Drugs and Drug Addiction (EMCDDA). Holland, one of the countries most tolerant towards cannabis, has no more hard drug use than most other European countries.

Beverly Fox of Seattle, Washington, suffers from the eye condition called glaucoma, and from severe arthritis. She believes that smoking cannabis clears her vision and greatly eases her pain.

What Is Drugs Education?

Until the 1980s, drugs education was virtually non-existent. But as recreational drug use among young people increased, countries such as the U.S. and Britain realized that young people needed to be taught about drugs.

A Los Angeles, California girl paints a mural as part of an anti-drugs project at her school.

INITIALLY, THE MESSAGE to children was very simple. They were told to avoid drugs at all costs. Very little was said to them about the differences between drugs, or why people might want to take them. However, at the same time children started to learn about drugs from different sources. Children's television programs, for example, began to explain how drugs could affect children.

How has drugs education changed?

In the late 1980s and early 1990s, experts in drug abuse were employed for the first time to oversee drugs education in schools. Since this time, the approach to drugs education has changed a great deal. The general aim now is to inform young people about the dangers of drugs, but also about the reasons why people might want to take drugs. Young people learn exactly what effects drugs can have. Sometimes, children are even taught how to minimize the risks to themselves if they do choose to take recreational drugs.

Drugs education can include many different approaches. One scheme that caused a lot of controversy was set up in 1997 by the Thames Valley Police in Britain. It involved taking 60 schoolchildren to Amsterdam, Holland to see the city's cannabis cafés and learn how the people who lived there coped with drugs. The police believed that straightforward and honest education would be the best way to keep young people away from drugs.

Other education initiatives around the world have included inviting drug addicts to classrooms to talk to children about what it is really like to have a drug habit. This first-hand information can be a powerful deterrent for children who are thinking of trying drugs. When Britain's teenage Royal Prince

Harry was alleged to have taken cannabis in January 2002, he was taken to meet drug addicts and learn about how drugs had damaged their lives.

Another recent approach is peer education, where young people with some knowledge about drugs talk to people of a similar age about the issues involved. Peer education can be particularly effective because young people are more likely to accept advice from those of a similar age, whose experiences of life are similar to their own.

There is a wide variety of balanced information available to young people, including helplines, leaflets, and websites. This booklet was produced in England by the National Health Service.

Early education

The American Council for Drug Education, one of the nation's leading anti-drugs agencies, urges schools to introduce drugs education at a very early age. It has compiled lesson plans, activities, and worksheets which can be used by children from age four up to seventeen. Activities for older children include learning about peer pressure and how drugs can affect a user's health and appearance.

national drugs helPline
0800 77 66 00

THE
SCORE
FACTS ABOUT
Drugs

plus info on gases, glues and aerosols

How do films portray drug use?

The first film to portray illegal drug use, *Reefer Madness*, was released in 1936. It depicted the smoking of cannabis as leading inevitably to insanity. Since then, many films have been released about taking drugs. In 1994, *Pulp Fiction* received rave reviews but also much criticism, as some felt that it glamorized heroin use. Two years later, *Trainspotting* dealt in more depth with the issues, and the result was a film which vividly highlighted the bad side of heroin use.

Since then, films such as *Boogie Nights*, *Blow*, and *Traffic* have explored the reasons for, and the results of, drug abuse. The increasing visibility of drugs in films suggests how much a part of modern society they have become. The hero of 1999's *American Beauty* smokes large amounts of cannabis, yet there were no negative comments about his drug use in reviews of the film.

Do role models have responsibilities?

Films which give a balanced view of drugs and their dangers could be said to be setting a good example. But some of those who star in them fail to do so. In 1994, the young film star River Phoenix died after taking a cocktail of illegal drugs. In 2001, Hollywood star Robert Downey Jr. was forced to leave the hit television show *Ally McBeal* after an arrest for taking drugs.

A scene from the 1999 film American Beauty *in which the smoking of cannabis is portrayed as an everyday activity.*

Robert Downey Jr. faces the press in July 2001, following a court appearance for cocaine possession.

Many famous and influential rock stars have also fallen foul of drugs laws. In the past, stars including the Beatles' Sir Paul McCartney and Mick Jagger of the Rolling Stones have been arrested for drugs offenses. The use of recreational drugs has always been seen as part of the "rock 'n' roll" lifestyle. But drug abuse has claimed the lives of stars—including Jimi Hendrix and Janis Joplin.

Do people in the public eye have a responsibility to act as good role models? Even the ex-president of the U.S., Bill Clinton, admitted to having taken cannabis when he was in college—although he claimed that he never inhaled!

DEBATE - Do famous people have a duty to set a good example?

- Yes. Famous victims of drugs include the singer Janis Joplin and the actor River Phoenix. These role models were guilty of setting the worst possible example to their fans and followers by getting involved with drugs and losing their lives through drug abuse.

- No. Drugs can affect anyone, rich or poor, famous or unknown. If young people see their idols' lives being ruined or ended by drugs, they will realize that it could easily happen to them. Nothing could be more effective in making young people choose not to take drugs.

Are We Hooked On Medicinal Drugs?

For thousands of years, people have been taking substances to relieve pain and cure disease. In the fifth century B.C., a Greek physician named Hippocrates used a bitter powder obtained from willow bark to ease aches and pains and reduce fever. The bark contained a chemical known as salicin, a similar substance to the active ingredient in modern aspirin.

TODAY, THERE ARE thousands of different drugs available, and they are used to treat numerous afflictions. Medicinal drugs can be divided into three categories: those that treat the symptoms of illness; those that are used in an attempt to cure illness; and those that prevent illness developing in the first place.

How do drugs treat symptoms?

Over the past century, there has been a massive increase in the drugs available to treat the symptoms of illness. In the past, the only effective drugs you could use for pain relief were those made from opium, which were highly addictive. The many painkillers available today

A woman outside a pharmacy in Germany opens her prescription. Medicinal drugs are easily available in modern society.

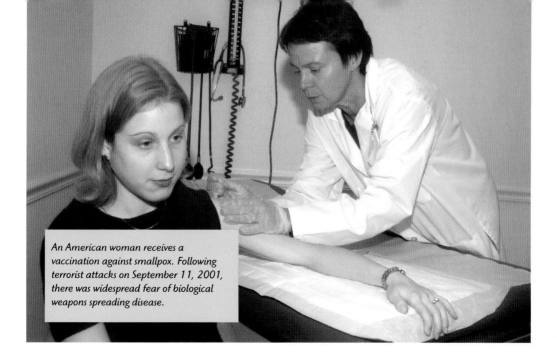

An American woman receives a vaccination against smallpox. Following terrorist attacks on September 11, 2001, there was widespread fear of biological weapons spreading disease.

include ibuprofen and paracetamol. Drugs have also been developed to combat symptoms such as nausea and high blood pressure. These drugs do not actually cure the problems, but they can make a huge difference to someone's quality of life.

What is penicillin?

The discovery of penicillin in 1928 by Alexander Fleming is considered the medical miracle of the twentieth century. Penicillin was the first antibiotic. Before this, there were no medicines to treat bacterial infections and diseases such as tuberculosis, which killed thousands each year. Since the arrival of antibiotics, millions of lives have been saved.

What is a vaccine?

During the twentieth century, vaccines were developed to prevent people getting diseases. A vaccine consists of giving a patient a very small dose of a particular disease, so that their body becomes immune to it. If they then come into contact with the disease in the future, they will not catch it. By the 1970s, the deadly disease smallpox had nearly disappeared due to a vaccination program. Today there are hundreds of vaccines available. These include drugs to prevent diseases such as measles, polio and flu. Scientists are even working on medicines to prevent people catching the common cold.

Prozac

Since it was introduced in 1986, the anti-depressant drug Prozac, which can help treat the symptoms of depression, has been taken by at least 38 million people. Prozac was one of a new range of anti-depressant drugs, which had fewer side-effects and were less addictive than their predecessors. Each year, Prozac's makers sell a few billion dollars worth of the pills.

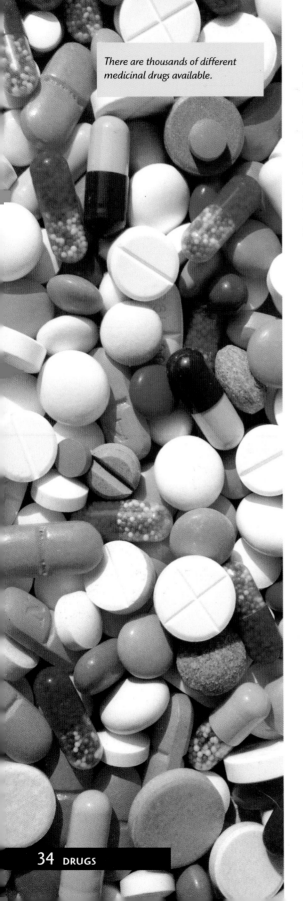

There are thousands of different medicinal drugs available.

Are medicinal drugs safe?

Everyone reacts slightly differently to the medicinal drugs they take. Some drugs work better for some people than for others, and some drugs are safer for some than others. Any drug that gets a license to go on the market has taken years to develop. This is why some drugs are so expensive when they are first released. When the anti-flu drug Relenza was launched on the British market in the late 1990s, it cost U.S.$33 for a course lasting only five days.

Although all medicinal drugs are tested vigorously, there are still questions over certain products. In Britain, scientists at the John Radcliffe Hospital in Oxford claimed in 1999 that over-the-counter painkillers such as aspirin and ibuprofen may be responsible for up to 2,000 deaths a year. They suggested that these can cause dangerous internal bleeding. Aspirin is perfectly safe for most people who take it responsibly. But for a tiny minority who cannot tolerate the drug, even one tablet can kill.

Many medicinal drugs are relatively safe if taken in moderation, but taking too many can result in death. Paracetamol overdose leads to more than 2,000 deaths worldwide each year.

Are medicinal drugs addictive?

In the U.S., a group of people launched a lawsuit in 2001 against the makers of the anti-depressant Seroxat. They claimed that when they stopped taking the drug they suffered disturbing withdrawal symptoms, including vertigo (fear of heights), agitation and confusion. Some people said that these effects were so bad they could not stop taking the drug.

In 1988, all British doctors were issued guidelines about the addictive nature of benzodiazepines (tranquillizers), saying they should not be given to patients for

Some people become addicted to medicinal drugs such as anti–depressants, which can cause more misery than the ailment they were intended to treat.

more than four weeks at a time. Even so, more than a million adults in Britain were hooked on this medication in 2001, prescribed for them by their doctors. Withdrawal from the drug can be as painful and as lengthy as that experienced by addicts who try to stop taking heroin.

Thalidomide

In the 1950s and 1960s, the drug Thalidomide was used to treat morning sickness in pregnant mothers. Tragically, the scientists developing the drug had not tested it thoroughly enough. Worldwide, over 12, 000 babies were born with defects, including shortened or missing limbs, as a result of their mothers taking the drug. Only 8,000 infants survived their first year of life.

Source: ABC News

This march in Durban, South Africa, in July 2000 was a protest at the high cost of drugs that can be used to treat HIV infection.

Will medicinal drugs change in the future?

As diseases change and people around the world are looking to improve their quality of life, the companies that make medicinal drugs constantly have to find new drugs to meet the demand.

In the 1980s, a terrible new disease called AIDS (Acquired Immuno-deficiency Syndrome) began to spread around the world. By 2000, there was still no cure, but pharmaceutical companies had successfully developed drugs which could lengthen sufferers' lives and even delay the onset of the disease among those infected.

Other illnesses, such as depression, have always been around but are becoming an increasing problem. The World Health Organization has predicted that by 2020, depression will be the second largest killer in the world. Not surprisingly, drug companies have reacted to this news by researching and producing ever more effective medicines.

Drugs are also being developed for complaints that are not a direct threat to health. The release of the anti-impotence drug Viagra in 1998 was good business for its maker Pfizer. In the first two weeks after its release, over two million prescriptions were written for Viagra in the U.S. alone.

Can antibiotics stop working?

An area of great concern for world health is the growing resistance of bacterial infection to antibiotics. These are widely used to treat illness in humans and animals, but overuse has led to some of them becoming ineffective against disease. Some bacteria have changed through contact with antibiotics, and the original drugs cannot now kill them. Developing new antibiotics is seen as one of the most important challenges facing pharmaceutical companies.

What is the cost of producing drugs?

Medicinal drugs are very expensive to develop. The companies that conduct the research on them get their money back by controlling the rights to produce the drug and by selling the drugs they produce. This has led to problems for poorer countries which have specific health problems.

In South Africa, there are well over four million people infected with HIV, the virus that can lead to AIDS. The government cannot afford the medicine to treat its citizens. But after much legal argument, pharmaceutical companies in the U.S. and Britain have agreed to let companies in South Africa copy their drugs and produce them at a much lower price.

In October 2001, a deadly disease called anthrax was deliberately spread in an act of terrorism in the U.S.. There has since been a fierce debate about whether governments should be able to buy cheap antibiotics to combat the disease from companies which do not hold the rights to produce them.

DEBATE – Should medicinal drugs be tested on animals?

In Britain in 1998, over two million tests were performed on live animals in licensed laboratories. Of these, about 52 percent were for medical research and drug testing. Should this testing continue?

- Yes. Human life is so important that it is vital to continue testing to help provide safe medicines.

- No. More effort should be made to find alternatives to animal testing. Animals have rights and feelings too.

Source: Home Office

A technician with anti-anthrax drugs. In October 2001, after a number of deaths from anthrax in the U.S., the Canadian government reached an agreement with the pharmaceutical company Bayer to produce the anti-anthrax drugs cheaply.

What are alternative medicines?

Alternative medicines are those drugs and treatments that are not part of conventional Western medicine. The medicinal drugs prescribed by regular doctors are generally produced by large pharmaceutical companies. Alternative medicines generally rely on more naturally occurring substances, such as herbs.

There are dozens of different alternative treatments. Herbal medicine is one of the most popular. Using different plants to treat complaints from circulation and digestive problems to depression and stress. Usually the bark, flowers, roots, or leaves of plants are used to make a medicine that can be eaten or drunk, releasing chemicals in the plant which may help the patient.

Homeopathy is another very popular alternative health treatment. Experts in this field, called homeopaths, give patients highly-diluted doses of carefully chosen chemicals which in larger doses could be poisonous. No one really understands why this form of medicine works, but millions of people use it everyday and say that it is extremely effective. Because the doses used are so small, most scientists agree that it is safe.

Are alternative medicines popular?

The World Health Organization estimates that about 80 percent of the world's population uses herbal medicine more often than modern medicinal drugs. Most of these people are from poorer countries, where it is much cheaper to obtain medicine from naturally-occurring plants. But these

Herbal remedies being sold at a market stall in China. Such remedies, containing plants, fungi and animal extracts, are particularly popular in China.

Hypericum Perforatum, *more commonly known as St. John's Wort, grows wild and is easily cultivated. It is a popular alternative treatment for mild depression.*

alternative therapies are also becoming more popular in the Western world. The number of alternative practitioners in the U.S. is rising steadily. In Britain in 1999, the British Medical Association found that there were actually more alternative practitioners than regular doctors.

Are alternative medicines safe?

Just because medicines are alternative, does not automatically mean they are safe. Herbal medicines can produce side-effects just as conventional medicines can. Indeed, many modern drugs are produced from the same plants. Are standards in alternative medicine always good enough? It takes years to become a regular doctor or to produce a new medicine. But anyone can claim to be an alternative therapist, and remedies are easily available for anyone to buy or sell.

Are Drugs Ruining Sport?

In recent years, the financial rewards for top sports stars have soared. But as sport has become big business, there have been increasing numbers of cases where sports stars try to succeed by taking "performance-enhancing" drugs.

THERE ARE MANY drugs that athletes can use to improve performance, most of which are banned by the various sporting authorities. Some banned substances, such as cortico-steroids, can help athletes by increasing levels of a natural painkiller in their bodies. This allows them to train harder. Others, such as human gonadic choriotrophin, can boost muscle growth and help recovery from injury. In the long term, these drugs can be very harmful.

Diego Maradona should be remembered purely as one of the world's greatest ever football players, but his name is also associated with drug abuse.

Of course, athletes sometimes take medicines just like everyone else, and they are allowed to take certain medicinal drugs. But even these can help improve performance—as can drugs such as caffeine, found in tea and coffee. This often leads to arguments about whether or not an athlete has deliberately cheated by taking drugs.

Who are the drugs cheats?

One of the most infamous drugs cheats was Canada's Ben Johnson. In the 100 metres at the 1988 Seoul Olympics, he won the gold medal and smashed the world record. Two days later, he was stripped of his medal after testing positive for anabolic steroids. After a second positive drugs test in 1993, Johnson was banned from competitive athletics for life.

Many other sports stars have fallen foul of drug use. In 1991, soccer star Diego Maradona was banned from the game for 15 months after testing positive for cocaine. He was then sent home in disgrace from the 1994 World Cup, after having been caught taking a banned stimulant called ephedrine.

Are drugs tests accurate?

In 1994, the British runner Diane Modahl was banned from competition for four years after urine tests showed a high level of testosterone in her body.

Cyclists in 1998's Tour de France protest at the way the press described the drugs scandal at the event.

Pedaling drugs

At the 1998 Tour de France, the world's most important cycling race, the extent of drug abuse in the sport was exposed. The leading Festina team was excluded from the competition, and its director admitted that drugs had been used to improve the performance of their cyclists.

Testosterone can enhance some athletes' performance, but Modahl insisted that she had not taken the drug. The next year, the ban was lifted after doubt was cast on the accuracy of the tests.

Many positive results for nandrolone, a banned performance-enhancing steroid, have been attributed to people taking dietary supplements or homeopathic medicines. In 2001, the Dutch footballer Edgar Davids used this excuse to explain the high levels of nandrolone found in his body—but he still received a five-month ban from the game. As performance-enhancing drugs become more sophisticated, it is increasingly difficult to identify the real cheats.

How Do People Stop Taking Drugs?

Many users do stop taking drugs of abuse, sometimes with the help of special treatment. But until the 1970s, the only way for most people to end their drug abuse was simply to stop taking the drugs. This was often very unpleasant, especially if the drug was addictive. Today, there are alternatives for those looking to kick their habit.

These Chinese women drug addicts are among the 800 inmates at a Beijing rehabilitation center.

IF USERS WANT to stop taking heroin, a doctor may offer them a synthetic medicine called methadone. This drug produces feelings similar to those produced by heroin, but it is not as strong or addictive. Addicts sometimes find it is a step towards giving up their dependency on heroin. Unfortunately, methadone also has side-effects, which are similar to those of the drug it replaces. If it is taken to excess, it can kill.

Professional counseling is one of the many tools used to combat drug abuse. It can be a great comfort for drug users to share their problem.

Kicking the habit

In Rajasthan, India, Narain Singh set up his first rehabilitation camp for opium addicts in 1979. Today, his center deals with about 60 addicts at a time, using group and spiritual therapy as well as light yoga exercises to help residents kick their drug habits. Singh claims a success rate of about 70 percent and is credited with having saved many lives.

Source: BBC Online

Scientists are working on other means to help drug addicts. They are in the process of developing a vaccine which they believe could help make cocaine users immune to the effects of the drug, making it pointless for them to take it. The drug, known as TA-CD, has undergone initial trials. If further tests are successful, it could be available to addicts within a few years.

Can rehabilitation work?

People who want to stop taking drugs often find it helps them to talk to a professional counselor. They can talk about why they took drugs in the first place, how to cope with withdrawal symptoms, and life after drugs. Sometimes, drug users are also placed in rehabilitation programs. These can provide a safe place for a few days or weeks, where there are no illegal drugs and there is plenty of counseling available. Courts have the option of sending convicted drug offenders into rehabilitation programs.

Worldwide, rehabilitation is considered an extremely useful tool for breaking the cycle of drug dependence. In 2000, the Scottish Executive announced that it was to spend U.S.$140 million to tackle the country's drugs problem, a substantial proportion of which would be spent on improving the country's rehabilitation facilities.

Is drug use really a problem?

In most countries around the world, the vast majority of the population does not take drugs of abuse. Even in Britain and the U.S., two of the world's largest consumers of drugs, most people have never taken them.

However, drug use is definitely a problem. In many countries, particularly in the Far East and Africa, drug abuse is on the increase. With drug abuse come the problems associated with it, namely crime and poor health. For those in any country who suffer from addiction, or for those who are the victims of drug-related crime, drugs continue to be an enormous burden.

This 1997 children's march in Greenville, South Carolina, promotes the view that life offers many better experiences and opportunities than taking drugs.

DEBATE – Should the use of recreational drugs be a personal choice?

- Yes. People should have the right to do whatever they like and take illegal drugs if they want to. What right does any government have to tell you what to do with your body?

- No. Drugs are not only dangerous for those who take them but can lead to crime which harms others. The authorities should take a tough line against drugs and their users, and encourage people to lead drug-free lives.

Baker's Chapel Elementary UNIT 24 supports

I'VE GOT BETTER THINGS TO DO THAN DRUGS

Red Ribbon Week 97'

Feeling fit

In the U.S. and Europe, over 10 million people are members of fitness centers. Those who attend fitness classes or go to gyms get a natural buzz from controlling their own fitness, losing weight and improving their health. Their bodies also produce chemicals called endorphins while they are exercising. This is a natural drug which helps them feel relaxed and happy for many hours afterward.

Why use drugs?

Young people can get enjoyment from life in a variety of ways. For some, studying is the most important thing in their lives, as they wish to get good test results and rewarding jobs in the future. Others play sport, which keeps them fit and can also be extremely rewarding. Activities like these can give a sense of achievement which is much more real and long-lasting than the artificial "highs" that any drug could ever give. Relationships with friends and family also give individuals pleasure and are another way in which people can lead meaningful lives. Drugs hold a strong appeal for some people. But they are never the only way to get something out of life, and they frequently lead to misery rather than enjoyment.

What Does The Future Hold?

No one knows exactly what will happen in the future. Will illegal drugs become legal? Will scientists find cures for the many killer diseases in the world? The only thing that is certain is that there will be changes in how we use and view drugs in our lives.

TWO HUNDRED YEARS ago there were no illegal drugs. Could it be that in another two centuries the same will be true? Cannabis laws certainly seem to be changing. Will all cannabis users be able to buy the drug in shops or bars soon as easily as smokers and drinkers can buy their chosen drugs now?

What about hard drugs? Legalizing drugs such as heroin and cocaine might reduce crime, but should society ever be seen to be condoning or encouraging their use? And what new drugs of abuse might be invented or discovered in the future? The past 15 years have seen the emergence of "dance drugs," such as ecstasy. In the next few years, an entirely new recreational drug might become popular. How might such a drug be used, and what part might it play in a future society?

Today drugs are part of the dance scene in Ibiza, Spain, despite the fact that they are illegal. In the future, will the use of drugs become more widely accepted, or will it be more strongly opposed?

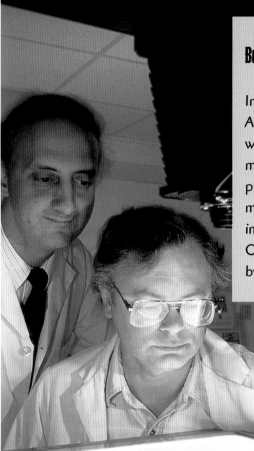

In his 1932 novel *Brave New World*, author Aldous Huxley describes a world in the future where everyone takes a drug called Soma, making them feel content. In a way, his prediction has come true. Every year, tens of millions of people use anti-depressants to improve their mood. The World Health Organization predicts that this figure will rise by millions over the next few years.

Scientists at work on a genetically-engineered AIDS vaccine. The potential cures offered by genetics are unlimited.

Will drugs change the world of medicine?

Scientists are constantly working to produce new medicinal drugs. Some are trying to develop drugs that can slow down the aging process. Others are looking for drugs to improve intelligence. And the quest to find medicines that can cure killer diseases such as cancer, HIV, and heart disease is the focus of huge amounts of work. Scientists are also finding new uses for medicinal drugs which have been around for years. Aspirin has been found to help fight heart disease—and even thalidomide, responsible for so many terribly deformed babies, is being hailed as a weapon against certain cancers.

Genetic engineering, with which scientists can alter the structure of living organisms, is certain to be an important factor in the development of new drugs. Scientists may become able to use genetic engineering to design their own drugs, which work in particular ways. There will then be virtually no limits to what drugs might be available to treat disease in the future.

The race has already begun to find drugs which can replace the antibiotics which are fast becoming ineffective in fighting disease. This, and other research into medicinal drugs, may become vital to our very existence.

REFERENCE

Drug Use

Number of People Using Specific Drugs Each Year (late-1990s)

	Number of people (millions)	% population (age 15+)
Heroin		
Oceania	0.6	0.27%
Europe	1.51	0.24%
Asia	5.74	0.24%
Americas	1.31	0.22%
Africa	0.57	0.12%
GLOBAL	9.18	0.22%
Cocaine		
North America	7.0	2.2%
South America	3.1	1.1%
Oceania	0.2	0.9%
Western Europe	2.2	0.7%
Africa	1.3	0.3%
Eastern Europe	0.1	0.04%
Asia	0.2	0.01%
GLOBAL	14.0	0.3%
Cannabis		
North America	22.2	7.2%
Africa	27.2	5.8%
Western Europe	17.4	5.4%
South America	14.7	5.3%
Asia	53.5	2.1%
Eastern Europe	4.7	1.5%
GLOBAL	144.1	3.4%
Amphetamines		
Oceania	0.6	2.9%
North America	2.2	0.8%
Western Europe	3.1	0.8%
South America	4.3	0.7%
Asia	2.1	0.7%
Africa	2.5	0.5%
Eastern Europe	1.0	0.4%
GLOBAL	24.2	0.6%

	Number of people (millions)	% population (age 15+)
Ecstasy		
Oceania	0.4	1.6%
Western Europe	2.3	0.6%
North America	1.2	0.4%
Eastern Europe	0.3	0.1%
Africa	0.1	0.02%
South America	0.02	0.01%
Asia	0.2	0.01%
GLOBAL	4.5	0.1%

Top Ten Countries for Drug Use each year, by Percentage of Population (age 15+), from Available Data

Cocaine
1. U.S.	3.0%
2. Dominican Republic	2.5%
3. Argentina	2.3%
4. Chile	2.1%
5. Honduras	2.0%
6. Guatemala	1.6%
7. Panama	1.6%
8. Ecuador	1.5%
9. Australia	1.4%
10. Spain	1.4%

Amphetamines
1. Australia	3.6%
2. Britain	3.0%
3. Honduras	2.5%
4. Philippines	2.2%
5. New Zealand	2.0%
6. Guatemala	1.7%
7. Taiwan	1.5%
8. Denmark	1.3%
9. Panama	1.2%
10. Nigeria	1.2%

Cannabis
1. Papua New Guinea	29.5%
2. Micronesia Federal State	29.1%
3. Ghana	21.5%
4. St. Vincent and Grenadines	18.6%
5. Australia	17.9%
6. Sierra Leone	16.2%
7. New Zealand	15.0%
8. El Salvador	9.2%
9. Britain	9.0%
10. U.S.	8.9%

Ecstasy
1. Australia	2.4%
2. Ireland	1.0%
3. Britain	1.0%
4. Spain	0.8%
5. Netherlands	0.8%
6. Germany	0.8%
7. Austria	0.8%
8. Denmark	0.7%
9. Belgium	0.7%
10. U.S.	0.5%

Drug Production

Opium Production Per Annum
(Tons)

1990

Asia

Myanmar, Burma	1,786
Afghanistan	1,730
Lao PDR	223
Pakistan	165
Vietnam	99
Thailand	22
Others (combined)	50
TOTAL	4,075

Latin America

Colombia	no data
Mexico	68
TOTAL	68

1995

Asia

Afghanistan	2,573
Myanmar, Burma	1,834
Lao PDR	141
Pakistan	123
Vietnam	10
Thailand	2
Others (combined)	86
TOTAL	4,769

Latin America

Colombia	78
Mexico	58
TOTAL	136

2000

Afghanistan	3,610
Myanmar, Burma	1,198
Lao PDR	184
Pakistan	9
Thailand	6
Vietnam	no data
Others (combined)	42
TOTAL	5,049

Latin America

Colombia	97
Mexico	23
TOTAL	120

Coca Leaf production per annum
(Tons)

1990

Peru	216,984
Bolivia	84,854
Colombia	49,935
TOTAL	351,773

1995

Peru	202,327
Bolivia	94,000
Colombia	89,186
TOTAL	385,513

2000

Columbia	242,440
Peru	59,849
Bolivia	14,767
TOTAL	317,156

DRUGS SEIZURES

DRUGS SEIZURES BY REGION (1999)

Region	Seizures (million units*)	Percentage of global	Units seized per inhabitant
Americas			
North America	7,328	32%	18.1
Caribbean	317	1.4%	8.6
South America	2,399	10.5%	7.0
Central America	193	0.8%	5.4
TOTAL	10, 237	44.7%	average 14.1
Europe			
Western Europe	6,401	28%	14.1
Eastern Europe	349	1.5%	1.0
TOTAL	6,750	29.5%	average 8.5
Oceania	63	0.3%	2.2
Asia			
Near, Mid-East, Southwest	2,279	10%	6.7
Central	286	1.3%	4.0
East and Southeast	1,670	7.3%	0.8
South	169	0.7%	0.1
TOTAL	4,404	19.3%	average 1.2
Africa			
Southern	753	3.3%	6.9
North	501	2.2%	2.9
West and Central	118	0.5%	0.4
East Africa	47	0.2%	0.3
TOTAL	1,419	6.2%	average 1.9
GRAND TOTAL	22, 872	100%	average 3.8

* A unit is defined as one dose of a drug.
For tablets, this is one tablet
1 unit of cocaine = 100 mg = 1.5 grains
1 unit of heroin or morphine = 100 mg = 1.5 grains
1 unit of amphetamines = 30 mg = 0.45 grains
1 unit of ecstasy = 100 mg = 1.5 grains
1 unit of cannabis herb = 500 mg = 7.5 grains
1 unit of cannabis resin = 135g = 2.025 grains
1 unit of LSD = 0.05 mg = 0.0075 grains
1 unit of methaqualone = 3.75 mg.

Sources: UNDCP World Drug Report 2000; U.S. State Department and the European Monitoring Centre for Drugs and Drug Addiction (EMCDDA)

GLOSSARY

AIDS (Acquired Immunodeficiency Syndrome) The final, life-threatening stage of HIV infection.

anabolic steroids Drugs that increase body tissue, especially muscle.

anesthetic A drug that causes loss of feeling, and can be used to numb pain or make a patient unconscious during an operation.

anthrax A potentially fatal bacterial infection.

anti-depressant A drug used to treat depression.

brand-name drugs Drugs which are made by a company and sold by a recognizable name.

contaminated Containing a substance that should not be there.

contentment A feeling of happiness.

convicted Found guilty of a crime.

dealers People who deal in drugs, buying and selling them rather than just having them for personal use.

decriminalize No longer treat an action as a crime, although it may still be officially illegal.

depressed Feeling extremely sad and unhappy.

diabetics People who suffer from the medical condition diabetes, where the body has trouble controlling levels of sugar in the blood and urine.

drug abuse The taking of illegal drugs.

environment An area or situation that you are in.

exhilaration A feeling of great excitement.

hepatitis A disease causing inflammation of the liver.

high A feeling of exhilaration after taking drugs.

HIV (Human Immunodeficiency Virus) An infection which destroys the body's immune system and can lead to *AIDS*.

inhale Breathe in.

insomnia Being unable to sleep.

insulin A medicinal drug that diabetics need to take because they are unable to produce it naturally in their bodies.

intravenous Into a vein, such as with an injection.

joint A cigarette that contains cannabis.

legalize Change the law so that doing something, such as taking drugs, is no longer illegal.

morning sickness A feeling of sickness often suffered by pregnant women.

opiates Drugs made from the opium poppy, including opium, morphine, and heroin.

organized crime Large-scale, coordinated acts of crime.

overdose The taking of too many drugs, which can send the body into shock or even kill the user.

peer Someone of the same age or social group. Peer pressure is when people feel under pressure to behave "like the others."

pharmaceutical To do with the preparing and manufacturing of medicines.

popular culture Entertainments enjoyed by the mass of ordinary people, such as television, fashion, and popular music.

prosecution The arrest and trial of a crime suspect.

psychological To do with the mind and the way people think.

recreational drugs Drugs which people use for fun or leisure.

rehabilitation Recovery, restoring to a condition where somebody can play a full part in the world.

relaxant A drug that causes a person's mind or body to relax.

rural In the countryside.

schizophrenia A mental disorder in which sufferers are confused, sometimes hearing and seeing what is not there.

side-effects Unwanted effects from drugs, which occur alongside the main, desired effects.

solvent A substance that dissolves another. Solvents include gasoline and glue.

stimulant A drug that speeds up physical processes.

stomach ulcer An open sore in the stomach, causing pain and bleeding.

Sumerian Relating to the ancient civilization of Sumer in Babylonia.

symptoms The signs that show when someone is ill.

synthetically Artificially, not naturally.

syringe A device with a needle, used for injecting drugs into someone's body.

trade figures The statistics showing how much money a country is making.

trafficking The transportation and trading of drugs between countries.

tranquillizers Drugs that make someone feel calm.

United Nations (UN) An international organization formed in 1945 to work towards the security and peace of the world.

United Nations Drug Control Program (UNDCP) A department of the United Nations which focuses on the world's drugs problems.

United Nations Office for Drug Control and Crime Prevention (UNODCCP) A department of the United Nations which focuses its work on drugs and crime.

withdrawal symptoms The unpleasant effects felt when somebody tries to give up a drug.

FURTHER INFORMATION

BOOKS

Facts About Alcohol by Ted Gottfried
    (Benchmark Books 2004)
Facts About Ecstasy by Suzanne Levert
    (Benchmark Books 2004)
Facts About Inhalants by Francha
    Menhard (Benchmark Books 2004)
Facts About Marijuana by Ted Gottfried
    (Benchmark Books 2004)
Facts About Steroids by Suzanne Levert
    (Benchmark Books 2004)
Series of books that aims to help young
adults make the right choices in
decisions that can effect their lives.

Issues in Drug Abuse various authors
    (Lucent Books 2005)

Teen Addiction (Lucent Books 2004)
Teen Alcoholism (Lucent Books 2004)
Teen Smoking (Lucent Books 1999)
Part of a series by various authors
dealing with Teen Issues. Appendices
include chapter notes, a glossary,
organizations to contact, and
suggestions for further reading.

Alcohol Abuse (Greenhaven Press 2003)
Club Drugs (Greenhaven Press 2005)
Drugs and Sport (Greenhaven Press 2001)
Titles in the *At Issue* series include a
wide range of opinions on a single
controversial issue. There are opinions
of eyewitnesses, scientific journals,
government officials, and others.

ORGANIZATIONS

American Council for Drug Education
164 West 74th Street,
New York, NY 10023
www.acde.org
The American Council for Drug
Education is a substance abuse
prevention and education agency that
develops programs and materials based
on the most current scientific research on
drug use and its impact on society.

Canadian Centre on Substance Abuse
75 Albert Street
Suite 300
Ottawa, ON K1P 5E7
www.ccsa.ca / CCSA /
tel: (613) 235 4048
Provides information and advice that
helps reduce the health, social, and
economic harm associated with
substance abuse and addictions.

Alcoholics Anonymous
Alcoholics Anonymous is an
international fellowship of men and
women who have had a drinking
problem. It is nonprofessional, self-
supporting, multiracial, apolitical, and
available almost everywhere. There are
no age or education requirements.
Membership is open to anyone who
wants to do something about his or her
drinking problem.
475 Riverside Drive
11th Floor
New York, N.Y. 10115
www.alcoholics-anonymous.org

Do It Now Foundation
0800 77 66 00
www.doitknow.org
Creates and disseminates accurate,
creative, and realistic information on
drugs, alcohol, sexuality, and other
behavioral health topics. Aimed mainly
at youths and students.

Drug Sense
14252 Culver Drive #328
Irvine, CA, 92604-0326
tel: (800) 266-5759
www.drugsense.org
A campaign group for drug policy
reform, which offers news articles and a
weekly newsletter and provides a forum
for debate.

**The National Council on Alcoholism
and Drug Dependence**
22 Cortlandt Street,
Suite 801
New York
NY 10007-3128
www.ncadd.org
email: national@ncadd.org
tel: (800) NCA-CALL (Hope Line)
An organization that fights the stigma
and the disease of alcoholism and other
drug addictions. It offers information for
students, parents, and health carers.

WEBSITES
**www.soberrecovery.com/links/
   narcoticsanonymous.html**
The website for Narcotics Anonymous
in the U.S. and Canada. It offers
information and details of meetings
nationwide for those with a drug
problem. There are also links to
international organizations.

www.nche.org/
The National Center for Health
Education in the U.S. aims to educate
people of all ages about healthy living.
Information is provided about drug use
and abuse and the risks involved in
taking them.

www.undcp.org
The official website of the United
Nations Office for Drug Control and
Crime Prevention.

**www.goaskalice.columbia.edu/
   Cat2.html**
Go Ask Alice! is the health question and
answer Internet service produced by
Alice! Columbia University's Health
Promotion Program—a division of
Health Services at Columbia. Search *Go
Ask Alice!* lets you find health
information by subject via a search of the
ever-growing archives containing nearly
3,000 previously-posted questions and
answers. *Ask Alice!* gives you the chance
to ask and submit a question to *Alice!*

www.drugworld.org
A multimedia website put together by
the charity Turning Point. It is aimed
primarily at young people and includes
harm reduction information.

INDEX